CARAVANNING IN THE 1970s

ANDREW JENKINSON

AMBERLEY

Dedicated to Mum and Dad, who gave me lovely memories caravanning in the 1970s,
making many friendships along the way

First published 2022

Amberley Publishing
The Hill, Stroud,
Gloucestershire, GL5 4EP

www.amberley-books.com

ISBN: 978 1 3981 1209 4 (print)
ISBN: 978 1 3981 1210 0 (ebook)

British Library Cataloguing in Publication Data.
A catalogue record for this book is available from the British Library.

Typeset in 10pt on 13pt Celeste.
Typesetting by SJmagic DESIGN SERVICES, India.
Printed in the UK.

CONTENTS

INTRODUCTION

The 1970s was a decade that had its ups and downs in many ways. The beginning saw generally cheap living, but by the middle of this decade the UK economy was suffering with inflation, job losses from old, dying industries, and an oil crisis, not to mention strikes. This book covers the whole decade, a decade I remember well, growing up in this new era which was often described as the 'pace-setting seventies'. My parents had bought our first family tourer in 1969 and we all took to caravanning like a duck to water. We were joining the growing ranks of this pastime. It was a time of great excitement in caravan design, tow cars and accessories, and caravan site development. This book contains many images from my archives along with my personal experience of caravanning in this decade.

My parents would carry on caravanning into the middle of November from early March, but many caravanners at this time called it a day by the end of September. So, if you were, like me, an eleven-year-old at the start of the decade who caravanned with his parents, this book will hopefully help you relive some of those times. Times when we sent postcards and listened to a transistor radio while playing Snakes and Ladders or Frustration, or Dad having his first morning cigarette while we all had a brew and ate chocolate biscuits before we made the beds up.

For those new to caravanning my book gives you an insight to how different the pastime was back in the 1970s. It was a time when you found out about a site by a guidebook or by visiting it, rather than by Google as you would these days.

Andrew Jenkinson
Caravan/motorhome/static caravan journalist and UK caravan historian
YouTube Channel: Caravan Industry Expert-Andy Jenkinson

The author, Andrew Jenkinson, on 22 January 1977 with his parents' then brand new 1977 Elddis Tornado – it had just been picked up that morning.

1

CARAVANNING FEVER GRIPS THE NATION

Let's rewind for a short time to the end of the swinging 1960s, a time when petrol was cheap and, well, prices didn't rise much at all. It was all pretty stable and also hire purchase was widely available. The 1960s had begun with a big increase in car ownership; the public wanted to go out for weekend drives and experience freedom with a car. Then there were the new weekenders who wanted to set off on a Friday afternoon and spend the weekend away, with many taking up camping as an economical alternative to hotels. The touring caravan was discovered by many in the 1960s, with small cars such as the Vauxhall Viva being used as a tow car. The caravan was to grow in popularity during this decade, with families being attracted to cheap weekend breaks and holidays with relative freedom.

The end of the 1960s saw caravanning growing; even small saloons like the Viva could tow this 3.8-metre-long Knowsley Juno.

The static caravan owner normally chose a site and area where they would stop for many years.

There was also the static holiday caravan user. They tended to hire or buy a static holiday caravan and pitch it on a site, then once sited it usually remained on that spot for years. A static could be also sited on a plot of land – usually a farm. The other caravan user was the one who went touring with their accommodation behind the car – this user was classed as a caravanner.

Fifty years previously, with the first car-pulled caravans in the 1920s, caravanning had been a rich man's pursuit. By the 1930s the touring caravan was more affordable, so the hobby began to grow. After the war and during early 1950s caravanning grew in popularity, especially with the launch of the Alperson Sprite caravan at a cost of £199 brand new – a cheap caravan made for the masses.

The 1960s would see caravanning hit new heights, with demand being met by new manufacturers in the UK. The end of the 1960s was a boom time for sites, dealerships, manufacturers and accessory manufacturers. This first chapter is the longest in the book and that's because so much was happening in caravanning at the start of the 1970s – caravanning fever had gripped the nation! I was aged eleven at the beginning of this decade and, with my parents buying their first caravan in 1969, I would personally experience this period (the 1970s) caravanning. It was a decade that would witness many changes.

At the start of the 1970s prices were pretty stable. House prices, for instance, increased, but slowly. Products didn't shoot up in price much either, and the oil producers were still selling the black stuff at a reasonable cost. Petrol was relatively cheap at 32p a gallon and fish and chips cost around 25p, while a pint of beer was around 12p or 14p. The good old

Myself posing by Mum and Dad's Welton caravan and Austin 1800 Mk2 car in July 1972 – ready for yet another caravanning weekend.

top-selling family car, the base Ford Cortina 1300 Mk 2, would set you back £914 in 1970; later in the decade that had risen to over £1,900. Top pop groups were T. Rex (my favourite) Sparks, Slade and The Osmonds, and TV was still largely in black and white.

The only real cloud on the horizon was the introduction of decimalisation on 15 February 1971. All of our old money gave way to the new 'easier' currency, but it caused confusion all round. I remember my parents saying prices will rise, as products were rounded up to the nearest converted figure so this would add extra costs. For me, though, personally the interest was the buzz of new manufacturers and new dealerships created in the early years of this decade. It wasn't uncommon for small garages selling petrol and a few used cars to start selling caravans – usually from a new small manufacturer.

H. C. Fawcett was a petrol station near York with a coach business stretching back to 1916. Around 1968 they sold a couple of caravans as a side business. By the early 1970s they had finished with coaches and had developed into a main dealership, becoming one of the early dealers for Swift Caravans and several other brands. House owners with attached land would sometimes be approached to sell caravans – small dealerships often started like this. Incidentally, one such dealer close to me was Dave Barron Caravans. The owner, Gordon Hold, had caravans for sale at the rear of the family home. Within just a few years Dave Barron Caravans had become a well-known dealership, having expanded quickly.

Other dealerships that started up from small beginnings were Campbell's in 1969, which was founded by Barney Campbell, who sold prefabricated garages and sheds. Also Goodalls, over in Huddersfield, which were the same; starting small, this family business sold caravans at weekends and soon expanded. Established growing dealerships that were southern-based included Maidstone Caravans, Jenkinson's Caravans (no relation to the author!), Hants & Dorset, Colin's Caravans and John Adams.

Above: H. C. Fawcett finished coach tours, but still sold petrol at their dealership near York – one of many petrol stations that took up caravan sales. (Photo courtesy of John Roberts)

Below: Ken Smith began the medium-priced Swift Caravans in late 1964 with his wife Joan and their son Peter. Swifts became sought after by caravanners in the 1970s. (Photo courtesy of Swift Group)

CAMPBELLS CARAVANS

LOSTOCK HALL, Nr. PRESTON

Telephone Preston 37269

Above: Many small dealerships began from home premises or spare land in the 1970s. Many would eventually close, while others would expand.

Left: Campbell's began by selling one caravan in 1969; by 1972 they had grown to a large dealership.

Lancashire's Leading Caravan Centre

Where else could you see the fabulous range of tourers including Cheltenham, Bessacarr, Stirling, Viking Fibreline, Cygnet, Panther, Lunar and Mardon

Best part exchange in the country

New for 1972 Beacon Fell Caravan Park, Longridge, Nr. Preston. Contact us as sole agents for full details of this new luxury caravan park. All amenities including mains water, mains electricity, licensed club, etc. See the fabulous range of Nene Valley caravans at the site or at Lostock Hall.

REMEMBER YOU SAVE MONEY AT CAMPBELLS

Jenkinson's were southern-based dealers and had depots at Taplow and near Earl's Court Underground station. They had been around for many years – another family business.

Larger group dealerships in this era were United British Caravans and the Gailey Group. Both of these were large concerns that would further grow in this period. Some dealerships were lucky to have an indoor showroom, which was ideal for viewing in inclement weather. It was also not unusual to have caravan dealerships within a few miles of each other, sometimes selling the same new brands too. Setting up as a caravan manufacturer in the 1970s was relatively easy to do too, especially in the East Yorkshire city of Hull. A good skilled workforce along with the docks meant Hull was ideal for timber imports as well as shipping caravans, with it becoming a booming export market.

Caravanning in Europe had taken off in a big way and UK-built caravans were affordable and stylish – more so than most foreign manufacturers available on the Continent. Willerby Caravans (based in the village of Willerby, just west of Hull) had begun in 1946 making beehives and packing boxes, moving to caravans mainly for living accommodation due to the housing shortage. Willerby had unknowingly, in 1946, essentially founded the caravan industry in East Yorkshire, especially around Hull.

Choose Gailey for Choice

The Gailey Group had opened branches from 1970, totalling twenty-two sales outlets by 1978. They usually took over established concerns.

CHOOSE Your CARAVAN UNDER COVER

AFTER YOU'VE SHOPPED AROUND YOU WILL STILL GET **A BETTER DEAL** AT

STEWART LONGTON CARAVANS

CHAPEL STREET, CHORLEY (Next to Railway Station) **Tel. Chorley 6035**

OPEN DAILY TILL 8 p.m.

Stuart Longton's at Chorley began in 1971 by the Hall family. They had a showroom that I remember visiting with my parents in 1972.

Willerby personnel would leave the company over time and begin their own caravan manufacturing business. Fred Robson was typical of this trend, leaving Willerby Caravans in 1957 and founding Welton, which produced luxury, hand-built caravans in Welton village. In the area in the 1960s others spawned too, such as Silverline, Ace, Belmont, Swift, Sovereign, Embassy, Royden, Minster, Riviera and A-Line Caravans – the whole area was vibrant. There were further new manufacturers popping up in other areas of the UK too, such as Elddis, Lunar, Fleetwind, Avondale, Panther and Fleetwood.

But it was the Newmarket-based Caravans International headed by Sam Alper OBE who built up the biggest leisure vehicle manufacturing company in the world by 1970. Ci's Sprite caravans were the group's best-selling brand followed by Europe (known as Europa by 1971), Eccles and Fairholme, with 30,000 tourers in total leaving the Newmarket complex in this period. Alper had expanded into Europe, buying foreign makes such as Danish maker OBI's awnings and German-produced Wilk & Stern caravans, as well as setting up new factories in Italy, Germany, Sweden, South Africa and USA.

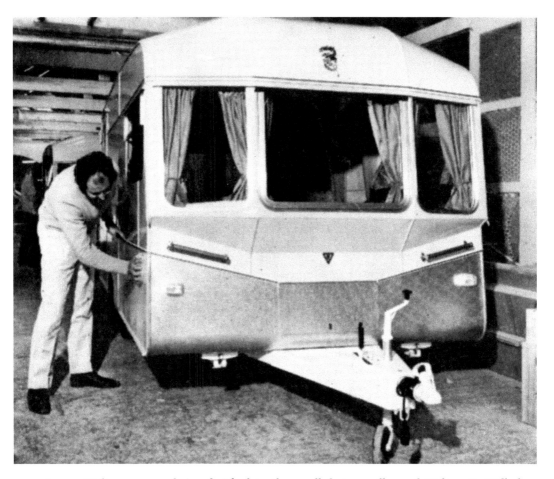

A 1971 Welton caravan being finished in the small factory village of Welton. Ex-Willerby employee Fred Robson set up Welton in 1958.

sovereign LEADS INTO THE 70s

See the Sovereign range of exciting, trend setting caravans. Whatever your preference there is a Sovereign just right for you !

★ Slim Sleek Appearance ★ Big Roomy Interiors ★ Comfortable Towing for Medium size cars ★ Spacious comfort for 4, 5 or 6 people ★ Supreme quality throughout in materials and craftsmanship.

A Brand New Range of Sparkling 10 Footers

CORONET 10 10ft., 4 berth £355
ORB 10ft., 2 berth with toilet compartment ... £370
SCEPTRE 10ft. 9in., 4 berth with toilet compartment £385

Above left: Hull saw factories built by new caravan manufacturers. Sovereign was the creation of Marfleet Joinery. Shop fitters and even coffin manufacturers entered caravan production, such was demand.

Above right: Lancashire maker Fleetwind produced low-cost caravans such as this 1971 Fleetwind 12 – the interior was the 14, costing £490.

Left: Sam Alper OBE would strive to bring better service and customer care for caravanners with his company, the Ci Group. He shaped caravanning in the 1970s.

If you caravanned in the 1970s, chances are your tourer would have come from this Newmarket plant. Ci produced 30,000 tourers annually in the early 1970s boom period.

Sam Alper had vision. He was a forward thinker and shaped the caravan industry to become more professional in its approach. Alper also gave the caravanner better service for parts and sales, and also issued proper owner's manuals, listing parts with each new Ci caravan sold. As caravanners began to travel further afield Alper had his overseas dealerships keep stock of all Ci parts, offering caravanners confidence with a Ci tourer.

Alper would promote caravanning too. Yes, of course, he promoted Ci brands, including the Autohome Motorhome Division and the Bluebird holiday caravan, but he also promoted caravanning overall. A big Ci stunt in 1970 was the Hover-Home, a European Bluebird caravan with twin engines that was ready to go into production but sales never materialised. Ci had tried this in 1968 with a Sprite Musketeer: it didn't go into production, but it gained lots of publicity for the Ci Sprite brand.

With your Ci tourer you received a proper owner's manual. Some manufacturers only supplied a small pamphlet.

Ci Bluebird hover home was designed to give caravanners access to more remote places, but it never went into production.

Alper knew that his efforts to promote caravanning would benefit Ci and profit from increased sales. Ci would publish several booklets explaining caravanning, which were handed out at shows as well as Ci brand dealerships. They explained costs and the equipment needed, and told you where to go and how to choose your first caravan – all Ci brands, of course. These booklets were produced in various formats from 1967 to 1974. Alper, though, would realise competitors would benefit from Ci's promotions, which Alper would address.

The booklets also covered touring into Europe, and I am sure this must have encouraged those already with a touring caravan to explore further afield, especially with the new improved ferry services brought into force at the beginning of the 1970s. The Continent was more easily accessible, with caravanners enjoying the sun and new vistas. The Caravan Club had a foreign service named Red Pennant with recommended sites and general information on caravanning abroad. Some caravanners ventured to the Arctic Circle and became members of the Blue Noses set up as a caravanners group. In 1970, one family wrote about their trip to Russia with their tourer and how they found the people curious during their adventure.

Caravanning abroad was popular. Italy, Spain and France were main attractions, with Belgium, Holland and Switzerland being other options. Caravanning friends of my parents in the early 1970s would set off in October for Spain. Once on their site the husband (a qualified electrician) would do jobs in the area where they stayed, earning money to pay for their winter sun. Come March they came back to the UK and were back out in the van again for weekends.

If you didn't want to take your caravan abroad you could, in some cases, have a self-hire drive and tow. Included in a package were flights and a car and caravan to use in countries such as South Africa. By 1970/1, Ci Group were manufacturing Sprites out in the States for a short time only, before the exercise was cut short due to high costs and a dent in Ci's

Right: Ci produced booklets from the late 1960s to early 1970s explaining how to buy, tow, load, and go touring, which were incredibly informative.

Below: UK caravanners flocked to foreign climes with caravan in tow. This is the Washington family's caravan in 1971 at Royan, France – they usually they went to Switzerland. (Photo courtesy of Peter Washington)

THE BOOK OF CARAVANNING

ci CARAVANS

turnover. However, while this US arm was operating Ci joined forces with BOAC in 1970 to enable UK caravanners to tour parts of the States using a Ci US-built caravan and an American car to tow it.

The cost was around £300–£400 and included a full tank of fuel plus a kitted-out, ready to go Sprite Musketeer, full insurance and flights. Another alternative in caravanning would come from a company in Nottingham who designed, manufactured and marketed a special GRP moulded caravan that could also double up as a boat to use on a canal or small lake. Named the Cara-boat, it was built from 1972 until 1974. Cara-boat had a Lombardi four-stroke engine that used a high-power six-jet unit, so no propeller was needed. You could sail on the canal in the comfort of your caravan, which you could then pitch up on a site as a caravan the next day – owners had the best of both worlds. Few were made, and many years later I saw one looking sadly neglected in a back garden.

Amphibious caravans were not a new idea; these types of designs had been around but had never appealed to caravanners, who didn't flock to buy a Cara-boat. Folding caravans was another niche market – again, an idea that had been around since the 1920s. The 1970s saw several folding caravans from small manufacturers. By the 1970s one make had a strong following and in modern times now have 'classic' status – Portafold. They were popular in this earlier period and cost £345. Folding caravans saw a sales increase,

Plymouth Satellite with a 1971 US-built Sprite Musketeer – you could hire one in conjunction with BOAC-Ci to tour the US.

UK-built amphibious tourer the Caraboat from 1972. This was to have limited success – it would probably never pass modern-day regulations. (Photo courtesy of John Lunn)

especially by 1974 when the fuel cost would rise. It was easy to tow and store, though these folders were a niche sector.

If you were not a Caravan or Camping Club member then there were plenty of private sites around. Publishers would print site guides on a yearly basis, while others were backed by *Modern Caravan* magazine. Information on facilities and costs was what the caravanner needed to plan holidays and weekend breaks. Guides like this were often kept in the car for easy access while touring.

With caravanning abroad becoming increasingly popular, some holidaymakers would opt to have a fridge fitted in their caravan. Back then the fridges were a lot smaller, so users were restricted on storage. Electrolux would prove the most popular fridge, costing from £37.75 in 1971. Another caravan fridge maker was Morphy Richards; however, Electrolux would become the market leader and innovator. The Electrolux ran on both gas and mains electrics (if available), but few sites/tourers had electrics fitted. As the decade progressed more caravans would have fridges fitted as standard, especially in luxury market models and later in entry-level models.

Site books had been around for years. *Modern Caravan* magazine produced this site guide, which included all commercial sites in the UK.

How did I manage without my Electrolux caravan fridge?

That's what thousands of caravan owners are saying these days. With an Electrolux 10 built into your caravan you too, can relax. No more spoiled food. Less eating out. No dashing to the shops every stop.

With an Electrolux 10, you can have all the food you enjoy at home. Fresh meat and milk. Crisp salads. Iced drinks.

The Electrolux 10 operates equally well along roads and lanes or at rest.

You can have it in a bottled gas version, or in a bottled gas/mains electric one.

Caravan kitchens can be hotter than ordinary kitchens. Can you honestly manage without the fridge you left at home?

See your supplier about an Electrolux 10 without delay. Or post the coupon.

Prices from £37.6.7. (recommended)

Fridges were becoming more popular with caravanners and the Electrolux 10, at just over £37 in 1970, ran off gas, even on tow.

1970s early caravan heaters for chilly evenings (or frosty mornings) consisted of gas open models, where ventilation was a must. They also caused the glass windows to heavily steam up and become wet – it was a problem with caravanners having small flannels on windows to catch the water droplets. Dad bought the Ubique gas heater, connecting it up to the floor-mounted gas tap with a rubber pipe. This heater was hot after being turned off for five minutes or more. Dad moaned about the amount of gas it used, we moaned about the windows steaming up and the dog yelped when it lay too close, the smell of burning dog wafting through the air.

If your caravan didn't have a gas tap as standard you could have one fitted at a cost of around £3 in the early 1970s. Modern caravanners could not imagine using a fire like this now, but most caravanners would, though only when very chilly. Alternatively, Dad would just light the gas hob to take the chill out of the air! The top and bottom of these were dangerous; you also needed good ventilation and couldn't leave on at night. The fire cost Dad £6 too, though he did a deal with the accessory shop since he had purchased two caravans inside three months from them.

A heater fitted with a flue was the answer. Morco heaters used this idea, but it was to be the Carver Truma heater that was to become the bestseller – it was efficient, had spark ignition and was reliable and easy to operate. Dad decided to have one fitted in our Welton tourer, which allowed us to use the caravan well into November, leaving the heater on during the night with safety. As the decade moved on blown air and thermostats were added to the Carvers, making them popular with caravan manufacturers to fit as standard.

Insulation in caravans was the norm and had been for some time, with the usual glass fibre matting used in the side walls and roof. Polystyrene sheets would become increasingly used in the beginning of the decade, which some claimed was the best type. Tin foil sheet was still being used with some smaller makers, but large Scottish caravan maker Thomson (T-Line) had their own ideas on insulating their caravans. They used mineral wool, but there were no firm reports as to if Thomsons were warmer tourers than the competition.

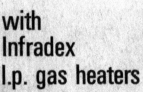

Out of this pile Dad bought the Ubique at £6 – what a discount! It caused condensation and cinged the dog.

THE CARAVAN HEATER THAT JUST CAN'T HELP BEING SO HIGHLY EFFICIENT

Carver Trumatic – the most advanced L.P. gas flued heater ever.

carver

Push-button instant heat that's completely safe and 95 - 98 per cent thermally efficient.

✱ Complete safety by a room-sealed system. ✱ Piezzo ignitor (no batteries). ✱ Flame-failure device. ✱ Size 18" x 16" x 4". ✱ Body finished in Beige and Coffee.

Every once in a while an appliance

By 1972 Dad invested into the Carver SB1800 fire, as did many caravanners. Shown here is a typical 1970s advertisement for it using a glamour model.

Underfloor insulation was an option but some luxury makers – such as Stirling, Welton and a few others – fitted it as standard. Dad's Welton had a sponge/foam material with polythene plastic sheeting to protect it. Later in the decade sandwich-insulated floors would be used.

By 1971 new caravans had red warning triangles fitted to the rear; by July 1972 this was law and all trailers and caravans had to display a triangle. So, as you can imagine, there was a boom in warning triangles sales as folk retrofitted them to older caravans and trailers.

In this period touring caravan hire had been around for some time, but it would be the 1970s that would see its popularity hit a peak. Many dealerships would carry around five caravans for self-tow hire, with larger dealerships having fifty plus, especially if the dealer had several outlets.

This form of holidaying was ideal for folk. A tow bar and electrics cost around £25 fitted, while a basic caravan such as a 3.90-metre-length four-berth Sprite Alpine, Monza 1200 or Perle 4/125 would be around £15–£25 a week to hire. At the end of the season hire fleets would be sold off at knock-down prices as the dealer upgraded to the latest models the following season.

HIRE A FULLY EQUIPPED TOURING CARAVAN and see the best of Britain and Europe

WRITE FOR CARAVAN HIRE BROCHURE

UNITED BRITISH CARAVANS

SALES CENTRES
- LONDON Colnbrook-By-Pass, Nr. West Drayton, Middlesex UB7 0HE. *Colnbrook 2606*
- NEWCASTLE Sandy Lane, Wideopen, Tyne & Wear. *Wideopen 3156*
- GLASGOW Fenwick Road, Giffnock, Glasgow. *041 637 6151*
- FRANCE Eurocaravanes, RNI St. Justin, 62170 Montreuil/S'Mer. *Montreuil 060365*

Right: You could hire a tourer at most dealerships. The larger concerns would run large fleets of Sprite models – UBC had a hire depot in France too.

Below: Caravan hire rates varied on size and season – back then it was big business for manufacturers as well as dealerships.

There were several tow bar manufacturers: Witter and Dixon-Bate, both based in Chester, were popular brands; while York, Tanfield, Ejector Exhaust and Eco were other makes of the time. Back then tow bar manufacturers didn't need any design approval, but Witter and Dixon-Bate were very keen on testing their bars and helped to set up approval standards for the towing bracket industry, which Witter would dominate. Famous tow bar makers such as Witter expanded their works to accommodate the growing number of new car models to design and make bars for.

When it came to the towing electrics, which in this period were simple, an auto electrician was needed. The Lucas Company, a massive UK auto electrical manufacturer and supplier to the car industry, also manufactured towing electrics, road lights, batteries and even 12-volt strip lights. Fitting a tow bar in those days in most cases meant drilling holes into the car's bodywork, but the seven-pin electrics were easy to fit, with a spare pin used for running interior caravan 12-volt lights from the car battery. Garages and most caravan dealers fitted tow bars, while others, like my dad and his mate, fitted their own; for example, Dad's Witter bar to his then new Ford Cortina Mk 3, though he left the wiring to an auto electrician.

In 1971, there was a caravan cookery book produced, aptly titled *Cooking for Caravanners*, which was backed by Ci and the forward was by Ci Chairman Sam Alper. The author, Anne Mason had originally emigrated from Australia to the UK in the 1950s with her husband, writing about travelling in Europe. Anne's talents stretched to cooking, and with her travel books she had a total of thirty books published. Some quite exotic dishes were included in *Cooking for Caravanners* and they could be cooked in most caravans. Of course, shots of Ci vans appeared in the book, promoting the Ci Group's brands. Ci ordered 25,000 copies of the book to be given in all new Ci vans sold in 1971/2.

The Witter works at Chester were busy in this period and manufactured their millionth towbar by 1975.

1. **Lucas fluorescent lights.** 8 and 13 watt fluorescent lights that run off any 12 volt battery and give as much light as you'd expect at home.

2. **Lucas electric water pump kit.** Complete with everything needed to make it work. And simple to fit.

3. **Trailer lighting set and reflectors.** All trailers or caravans must have triangular reflectors, by law. If they're over 5 metres long, they need amber side reflectors, too.

4. **Caravan and trailer lights.** 12 volt, stop, tail and flasher lamps, number plate lamps and front marker lamps.

5. **Lucas Karaflash kit and KF2 flasher conversion kit.** The KF2 flasher uprates a car's flasher system to cope with the extra load from a trailer or caravan. The Lucas Karaflash kit also includes a seven-pin socket complete with mounting bracket.

6. **Lucas Fireball battery.** Run caravan electrics from a new Lucas Fireball. Light, portable and clean. A freeze-start battery with an 18 month free replacement guarantee.

7. **7RA split charging relay and 4DB blocking diode.** For charging an extra 12 volt battery from a car's generator.

8. **7-pin plug and socket.**

9. **Wiropax cables.** Available in 6 amp (18 ft) and 17.5 amp (8 ft), complete with two Lucar connectors and two bullet connectors.

10. **Lucas 560 low voltage connectors.** A 560 connector joins wires without soldering or stripping them.

The things we do for you.

LUCAS

Joseph Lucas (Sales & Service) Ltd.,
Great Hampton St., Birmingham B18 6AU.

Above: Lucas once supplied all caravanning electrical components in the 1970s.

Right: Some caravanners fitted their own towbars, though back then drilling into the car's bodywork was usually the case with the fitting.

The 1970s could be really classed as beginning at the back end of 1969, with the then major caravan show in London at Earl's Court. This was the show that displayed what was on offer for the following year, which was 1970 – the start of caravanning in the 1970s. Crowds gathered (120,000) to get into the Earl's Court International Caravan & Camping Exhibition. Salesmen in those heady days at Earl's Court often had folk lined up for a new caravan. They would swap over with a colleague to have a break and carry on signing up such was the demand to buy.

The cost to get into the exhibition was 5s (25p) for adults and 3s 6d (17p) for children. New and old caravanners were eager to see what was going on in the world of caravans, caravanning and camping. The show boasted a shopping complex with the latest in caravan accessories and forty caravan manufacturers and, for the first time, six motorhome manufacturers were exhibited. There was a centre attraction with an outdoor camping display and you could test your skills in towing indoors.

Scotland had its own version of this with Kelvin Hall in Glasgow, while Birmingham had Bingley Hall, but by 1976 this was at the new NEC. The Birmingham show was held at the start of the year and Glasgow's Scottish show was held once every two years – the 1970 show had an attendance of 79,555. For years both shows would be dealer supported with manufacturers not being present.

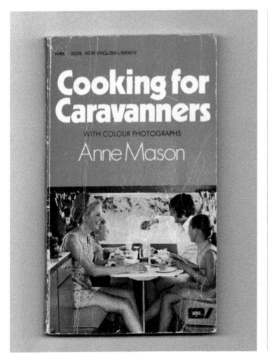

Above left: Just what caravanners needed, a dedicated caravanners cookbook (another Ci idea). One was given with each new Ci tourer sold in 1971/72.

Above right: The London Earl's Court show was the one that kicked off the new model year and where our decade begins.

Earl's Court attracted around 120,000 visitors. There was plenty to see and buy, including large accessory displays such as seen at this Gailey stand.

From Bingley Hall, Birmingham, this local caravan show would by the mid-1970s move to the NEC, where dealers such as Gailey supported the show.

The London show was the main shop window of the caravan industry, and overseas buyers came to this all-important showcase. New models and makers attended this show run by the National Caravan Council and the *Daily Mail*. Caravanners had lots to see at Earl's Court with all the different layouts available. The most popular layout was the 3.95-metre-length layout with front dinette, side kitchen, wardrobe opposite and side settee with bunk above and corner washroom. For years this design was used, also being stretched into 4.5 metre lengths too.

The most popular layout in the 1970s was in a 3.8-metre-length sleeping four. This is a 1973 Ace Pioneer family four-berth, medium-priced model at £670 – one of many makers using this layout.

Earl's Court was dominated by the UK's biggest caravan manufacturer, Caravans International, with a large stand and brand new models for 1970 on display. This included the new, redesigned Sprite range and two brand new Eccles and Fairholme models. In the latter part of 1969 the company had put their newly designed 1970 Sprite Alpine prototype (the UK's top selling tourer) on an endurance run around the famous Monza racetrack in Italy, breaking speed records for towing.

Ford supplied a Cortina 1600E and a Ford Corsair 2000E towing a Sprite 400 and Sprite Alpine at average speeds of 60 mph. At the show, rally driver Liz Firmin brought onto the Knowsley stand a Knowsley 3.2-metre-length Eros four-berth model that she had towed to London and Athens non-stop, covering 2,014 miles in 47 hours and 40 mins. Fresh from the run with her Reliant Scimitar, Liz related stories of hairpin bends, Alpine gradients and rough tracks. The caravan's durability was tested to the limit. Liz remarked on her arrival at the show: 'You can keep your test tracks, desert crossings my test was the real thing!' She won the Caravanner of the Year award in 1969/70.

Towing endurance runs had been going on since the 1920s, with Eccles then leading the field. Lynton caravans went for a towing record using a Ford 'super' Transit 5 litre, towing a straight production Lynton Arrow tourer fitted with uprated tyres. The speed attained was 103.09 mph. The 1970s would witness more Ci endurance tests to prove that caravans were easy and safe to tow.

The 1969 Earl's Court show was buzzing with news about Ci's 'caravan designed for the 1970s and beyond'. It was a bold statement, but the new models from its Eccles and Fairholme brands were striking tourers by the Ogle design team headed by Tom Karen of Raleigh Chopper, Reliant Scimitar and Bond Bug design fame. These new designs were to appeal to non-caravanners to prove how advanced a caravan could be. Plastic mouldings

Right: Rally driver Liz Firmin towed a Knowsley Eros, 3.2 metres length, in November 1969 from London to Athens in 47 hours, covering 2,104 miles.

Below: Lynton Caravans used a supercharged 5-litre Transit van to test stability at speed with a straight production model.

were used in the two models' construction and, with a higher-than-average specification, they had kerb appeal and novel yet unpractical ideas, such as a chassis that ended at the axle line with wooden battens to support the rear caravan bodywork.

The early part of this decade saw demand for sites at an all-time high as caravanning boomed. The touring caravanner was in need of more sites to accommodate the growing numbers. Roads were to become busy in summer, with touring caravans holding up local traffic especially in favourite holiday locations. Discussions were held with local authorities to see what could be done. Some local councils complained caravanners spent little in local areas – it was thought they brought their own supplies with them and often had meals in the caravan, pulling off into a back road, finding a spot to pitch up and perhaps staying for several nights.

Above left: Ogle Design were brought in by Ci to design a new generation of tourers for 1970. This is the Fairholme 425, which cost £665 and came with a fridge, shower and oven.

Above right: The Eccles Amethyst was the sibling to the 425. It received far more limelight and success, influencing Eccles' other models by 1972.

Left: Caravanners could stop overnight at pull-ins, like my parents did, saving a few bob on site fees.

A common sight in summer: caravanners off on touring holidays. Some motorists accused tourers of clogging up roads.

Of course, the growing sector of sites in this early part of the decade was the role of the Caravan Club (the Caravan and Motorhome Club, as they are known today), who were to open new sites with their members in mind. In 1970, around 80,000 members belonged to the club, but by 1972 this had swollen to 100,000. The club published a site directory each year, which included some non-Caravan Club sites that were approved by the club. There was also the Certificated Location site (CL), which in 1971 had over 2,000 listed. These sites usually had a limit of five touring caravans for no longer than twenty-eight days' stay.

Some were basic with just a tap in a field for water and a place to empty the loo and waste water. They were inexpensive and my parents used them all the time. A particular favourite was close to a river on a farm; what fantastic weekends I spent there fishing and making friends with the local kids. I learnt how to drive a tractor at twelve! Mum and Dad made friends with other caravanners on this CL and it became a sociable weekend's caravanning. I have memories of being out in the fresh air and playing football and cricket, making rafts and exploring local woods – great times.

Many CLs were set in super locations and also cost less than a fully serviced site, which could be up to 50p a night per person. My parents loved the Yorkshire Dales, going on several touring holidays, but again using CL sites. The club also organised regional

Left: The Caravan Club, as it was known back then, welcoming its 100,000th member, who received free membership and other perks.

Below: A typical CL site of five tourers. These were placed in some lovely locations and usually offered basic facilities.

membership sections throughout the country. Counties were split into north and south sections. Rallies for these were organised for weekends or longer by members at various locations and would have sixty-plus caravans attend. Rallies were a way for fellow caravanners to get together, with many friendships formed lasting years. Games and entertainment were part of the course. Gathering round the flag for drinks or a BBQ made these events very sociable.

The sections of the club would all come together once a year for the National Rally event, which attracted a big turnout no matter what the weather. The Caravan Club would bring in

Right: Mum and Dad's Welton and Cortina at Clapham, North Yorkshire, on a CL farm site in 1976. CL were a favourite for my parents, and for others too.

Below: Caravan Club rallies were popular and sociable events, and by the 1970s were attracting large weekend turnouts.

top entertainment, including shows and live performances. It was – and still is – a large calendar event. In the early 1970s the best home-built caravan competition held at the National Rally would come to an end – a sign of the changing times. A section of the club that had been well supported with DIY builds in days gone by; in fact, Elddis Caravans were basically established from this event when Siddle Cook's home-built caravan won in 1963.

If you still wanted a DIY caravan project you could buy one of several glass-fibre caravan shell's available to fit out. Yes, this was a niche sector. Vanmaster GRP shells were the most popular, but several other makes were available. Vanmaster shells had sold steadily at one time, fitting them out as a completed caravan too if desired by Vanmaster themselves. By 1977 production ended as DIY caravan making had dried up. With the amount of caravan manufacturers around, loyal owners of a brand would often form an owners club. Small, one-brand rallies during the season were organised, with owners often invited to factory tours and input from them proved helpful to the design teams of the brand. Owners clubs would sometimes exist for years after the company had finished.

This early part of our decade would also witness the continuing popularity of caravan rally road racing! This event began in 1954 and by the early 70s was a full on event with

Gordon Wareham's home-built caravan cost £650 to make in 1971. The home-built Caravan Club competition was to finish by 1973.

Above left: GRP caravan shells for DIY fans were a niche 1960s/70s market. Vanmaster were the most popular, making 3.80-metre- and 4.41-metre-length variants.

Above right: Owners clubs were popular by this period. This is a corner of the luxury Safari Caravans owners weekend rally.

other events such as the Red Rose Rally splitting off from the main British Caravan Road Rally held around early April. Caravans were tested to the limit on public roads and on racetracks. This practice could never happen in modern times due to safety laws; but later in this decade restrictions would be put into place. Caravans became badly damaged usually hitting a tree down back lanes.

Manufacturers backed teams and spectators could be sure of exciting moments as caravans hurtled down small back lanes in the early hours, while track sections tested driver and outfit to the edge. Many caravans were written off and those that survived would be judged in a concours for best condition outfit. Ci and Witter were big supporters, along with Bailey, Thomson, Elddis, Trophy, Bessacarr, Lynton, Swift, Robin and Silverline, plus caravan dealers and private entries. Some caravans were so badly damaged they had to be roped to keep them from falling to bits.

Another idea was (and, yes, we're back to Ci for this – told you they were forward thinking) to have around twelve new cars in 1971 with tow bars and test them at Chobham military test track with different Ci tourer brands matched to the various models, publishing results. This press event was designed to help new tow car buyers choose an ideal vehicle for the job. Performance was measured and evaluated at the testing track under strict conditions. Caravanners' top tow cars in the early 1970s were typically the Triumph 2000, a popular choice, with Volvo's 144 being another favourite.

The British Caravan Road Rally had become a major event. The Witter team's Triumph 2000 and 1972 Sprite Alpine hurtle down a forest track. (Photo courtesy of Witter Towbars)

Peter Smith, chairman of Swift, putting a Swift Silhouette through its paces on a track section. (Photo courtesy of Peter Smith – Swift Group)

Above: This 1972 Eccles Topaz has taken a punishing time and strapping held the rear to the chassis.

Below: Ci held a press day of towing with around twelve cars and Ci matching caravans to see which cars were good for towing.

The Range Rover was a caravanner's ideal tow car, but they cost £2,000 new when launched.

The BMC Austin and Morris 1800s were also good tugs. Dad had owned two and loved the fact that the suspension could be stiffened at the rear with the car having BL's Hydrolastic fluid suspension system. Even the BL Austin Allegro, as a small tow car, found favour with caravanners. Other rated tow cars were BMC's Austin Maxi 1500, but a 1750 engine also became available, adding to its tow car ability. The Range Rover launched in 1969 was to prove a first-class tow car for those caravanners who could afford one at nearly £2,000, but they were an option for those with a large heavy tourer over a Land Rover.

The Cortina Mk 3 was a decent tow car, especially as most people owned one (it was a company car favourite) and found them satisfactory. Even smaller cars such as the Vauxhall Viva/Ford Escort could tow smaller caravans. Most cars of the day had soft springs, and heavy nose weights on caravans produced a U-shaped outfit with the front of the car pointing skywards. Also, soft suspension caused pitching on uneven roads, though I can't ever recall roads back then being full of potholes like today.

The Cortina Mk 3 was a popular towcar with several engine choices.

Towing aids were available to help avoid the problem seen here by making the suspension stiffer.

Various ideas were tried to improve towing stability; for example, stiffening rear suspension using various aids and shock absorbers, which included stabilisers such as the Scott design that many caravanners used with success. The idea was to keep caravans from snaking and pitching, cutting potential accidents. Loading up your caravan was always detrimental to stability and not being nose heavy. Dad kept weighty stuff in the seat bases and over the axle, which aided stable towing. New caravanners would have a list to tick off what they were taking and where items could be stored for correct balance for this purpose.

Caravan parks were slowly improving, but old sites from after the war still could be found – usually with old static tourers with overgrown grass and a small shed with a

First time caravanners often made a list out for an outing. Here Dad ticks off his list, using his copy of *Practical Caravan* to lean on.

loo. These sites would be usually shut down and the land sold for building, or eventually receive investment to improve pitches and facilities. There were often small caravan sites placed behind privately owned petrol stations – a common feature in the 1970s. Some were pleasant but others were quite grim, with overgrown weeds, no proper pitch and poor toilet facilities. My grandparents would stop on one of these petrol station sites visiting friends near Doncaster. Dad would tow our caravan for them to use. They had stopped at this garage site with their own caravan in the mid-1950s early 1960s.

Back then caravanners towed smaller caravans than today. In the early part of the decade a 3.8-metre caravan was the standard size, usually sleeping up to five and having a loo compartment – well, a little room that you could put your loo in. And that was a basic Elsan design, fill it and chuck it types, though posh folk had a flush model by Thetford. Named 'the Porta-Potti', it was pump-flushed by hand.

Caravan magazines of the day published site reviews, and reports on new caravans and cars and general caravanning events even tested loos. *Caravan Magazine*, *Practical Caravan* and *Modern Caravan* were popular publications with tips and reviews of new caravans and products. These magazines were the caravanner's Bible, with *Practical Caravan* becoming the overall bestseller on news stands.

There were still small commercial sites like this, usually behind a petrol station and often on a bit of overgrown land.

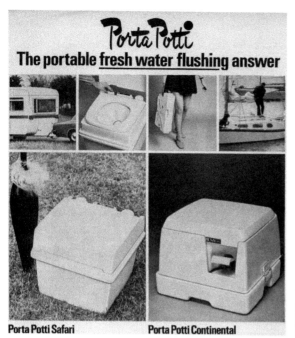

Porta Potti

The portable fresh water flushing answer

Porta Potti Safari   Porta Potti Continental

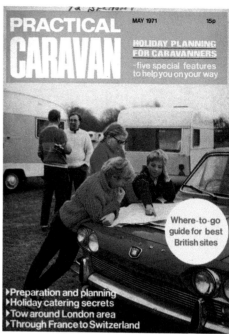

PRACTICAL CARAVAN

MAY 1971   15p

HOLIDAY PLANNING
FOR CARAVANNERS
–five special features
to help you on your way

Where-to-go
guide for best
British sites

▶Preparation and planning
▶Holiday catering secrets
▶Tow around London area
▶Through France to Switzerland

Above left: Thetford's loo had a hand flush and emptying cassette section, and was branded 'Porta Potti'.

Above right: *Practical Caravan* was to become the leading magazine for caravanners.

Caravanning was a cheap holiday for many, but like any hobby it can be cheap or expensive depending on equipment. For some a caravan was also a status symbol and they wanted the best luxury caravan money could buy. There were small niche caravan builders who used the best materials and would also build to customers' requirements. These luxury brands were usually traditional inside and out. They were built by skilled craftsman with attention to detail. It was a market that would be on the wane by this period, but there were still older buyers for this type of caravan. Carlight was the main luxury maker, with hand-built models from £1,090 to £1,990 in 1971.

Other makers in this period were Stirling, Safari, Royale, Welton, Castleton, Viking, Cheltenham, Buccaneer, Ensor, Bessacarr, Carapace, Sinclair Gordon and Embassy, who catered for the luxury buyer. The makes Carlight, Royale, Stirling, Safari, Viking, Cheltenham and Ensor were a bit old fashioned in design, but the quality was superb. These expensive caravans were usually locked on a dealer's forecourt, only opened to a serious buyer. By 1971 Dad had moved to the 'clubman' caravan, with a new 1971 Welton Rosaleda costing £695. Some caravan snobbery crept in: 'I feel king of the caravanning road,' Dad remarked with the Welton on tow.

This was the period when the awning that had once, for many caravanners, been more of a luxury accessory was now becoming more affordable. With names such as Harrison, Raleigh, Poulard and Spacemaker, this expanding market would be joined by foreign

Luxury Kay & Fryer Carapace caravan under construction. Luxury caravans such as these were for caravanners wanting the best they could afford.

Interior of a Carlight Casetta two-berth, super luxury tourer in 1971, which would have cost £1,070.

Hand-crafted luxury tourers like this Royale 1475 had appeal to traditional buyers wanting status in caravanning circles and top quality.

imports. Isabella was a new name from Sweden that soon earned a foothold in the UK in the early 1970s with quality design and manufacture. OBI was another imported awning, this time from Denmark, which would become owned by the Ci Group.

Awnings enabled extra space for further dining or sleeping areas or additional storage. They were becoming easier to erect and several awning makers also made toilet tents for caravanners who lacked a loo room in their tourer. Sites would need to accommodate the growing awning boom with pitches made larger for awning users. Some awnings could be hard to erect but this didn't hold back their growing popularity. The average caravan width was around 2 metres then – narrow by modern standards – so normal pitches were often too small with an awning put up.

Special awning-only pitches began to be added on larger sites, charging extra for the privilege. Many sites still operated on a 'pitch your van where you wanted' concept, as long as it was relatively straight and not too near others. So, awnings were not encouraged by some site owners due to space, and awnings killed the grass too. Dad once looked at an awning, but we just knew it would not be a great idea for us – he wouldn't have had the patience to put it up!

If you had a heater you could use your tourer from early in the season to later on – most caravanners back then put their caravans into storage by early October and began again in April when sites reopened. I remember one Easter with my parents in the Yorkshire Dales

Isabella Awnings from Sweden offered quality designs and by the mid-1970s were on most buyers lists for caravan awning.

With an awning caravanners could use it as a good-sized extra lounge or sleeping accommodation.

With the increase in awning ownership caravan sites made pitches larger for awning users or made pitches in general larger as demand increased.

Some sites didn't take awnings due to the pitches being close together. (Photo courtesy of Peter Washington)

waking up very cold with snow outside. That's when the gas fire was brought into action, or Dad would put the twin hob gas burners on. Mum made blanket liners for our sleeping bags in an effort to keep warm. If you caravanned at this time of year and in hilly areas, snow could not be ruled out. By 1970 onwards caravan manufacturers were fitting gas bottle lockers on the front drawbar, but if you had a basic tourer with no gas bottle locker you could buy gas bottle covers for the dumpy cylinders to protect them and stop the gas freezing up in cold weather.

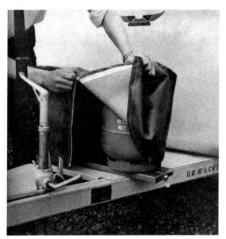

Above: Most caravanners laid up their tourer for the winter months at a storage site, some of which were just a yard with chain across the entrance.

Left: If your tourer didn't have a gas bottle locker you could purchase these special covers to protect the bottles.

With early Easter caravanning, snow could not be ruled out, especially in hilly areas like this site in 1972 near Bala. (Photo courtesy of Peter Washington)

Sitting in the caravan during the evening after a day out, entertainment was limited. It was a case of a transistor radio and a collection of board games or cards as the gas lights hissed. Meals in caravans were often quite formal; my mum insisted on 'laying the table' in the caravan with cups and saucers, plus a proper teapot. Socialising in the evening would involve a packet of biscuits coming out of one of the few roof lockers and Mum brewing a pot of loose-leaf tea. We all had cups and saucers – no mugs. This is how my parents and their caravanning friends spent an evening, usually participating in a game of cards too – often whist or gin rummy.

The advent of the transistor would see Japanese radios flood the UK market and although small portable TVs had been around since the 1960s, their poor performance and small, 9-inch screens meant sales were low. It would be the early 1970s that 12-volt portable TVs began to really hit the market. These proved ideal for the caravanner, using the car battery as well as mains power source for home use. My parents bought their first portable TV in 1971 – an Elizabethan 14-inch black and white set, one of many sets available at this time. It cost £80 and we could now watch telly in the caravan – if we could get a TV signal, that was! TV aerials would begin to appear on touring sites – many on an aluminium pole clamped to the van's drawbar. But, as many kids, all I wanted to do was find some other kids to play with. If the site had space to play some games by the pitches it wasn't long before two football teams were formed, or other ball games were played. I loved meeting other kids on sites – it was all part of caravanning.

Above left: Photo by Mum in July 1970, showing her neatly laid out caravan table set through the window. Caravanners laid the table as they did at home.

Above right: Dad purchased this portable TV model – a 12-inch screen complete with detachable anti-glare filter. It cost £75 from a local electrical store.

Some sites had enough room to play games between caravan rows, but few had designated ball game areas.

After buying a new portable TV caravanners could watch popular sitcoms of the day, such as *Dad's Army*, as long as the battery was fully charged. In 1971, *Blue Peter* were fundraising for underprivileged children who didn't get a holiday. The presenters asked viewers to send in knives and forks (did you do this?). 200,000 were needed, and within weeks they had raised enough cash to buy three eight-berth caravans (Beverley Coach Craft 625s) to place on three parks in Aberdeen, Blackpool and the south coast. The caravans provided underprivileged children a holiday through the summer.

Several celebrities caught the caravanning bug too. In 1972, Andrew Gardener, the ITV newsreader, purchased a new 1972 Ci Fairholme tourer from Maidstone Caravan Centre. He planned to tour Europe with his family. In the 1970s TV actor Victor Madden and his wife became keen caravanners, his image being used for various caravanning accessories. England goalkeeper Peter Bonetti became a caravanner in 1972 with his family of four kids.

Right: Watching TV in the van was becoming more popular, though we doubt the telescopic aerial would have been much good.

Below: The *Blue Peter* caravans for underprivileged children bought with old knives and forks sent in by viewers – I remember these being in the studio.

Dame Shirley Bassey also took up caravanning in the mid-1970s, buying a luxury Lister Salamander. Celebrities taking up caravanning influenced new interest in this leisure activity.

In this early period there was an alternative way of caravanning – cara-sailing on a canal. Known as 'trailer sailing', a flat-deck boat was easy to load your caravan onto. The boat had a 65-gallon water tank and you put the caravan's pump in, plus a 12-volt battery, and off you went. The company operated by Bradford Boat Services hired out two boats on a weekly charge of £24 to £37 a week. The boat chugged along at walking pace using a Lister

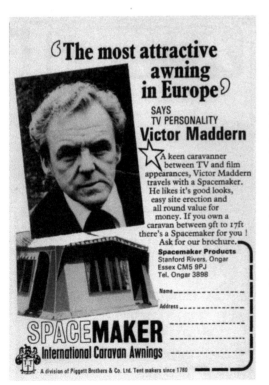

Above: TV newsreader Andrew Gardener with his family collecting a new 1972 Fairholme Goldfinch with his Volvo estate to tour abroad from Maidstone Caravan Centre, Kent.

Left: Victor Madden was a well-known actor. He was a caravanner too and advertised for Spacemaker Awnings in 1972.

Opposite above: Goalkeeper Peter Bonetti and his family pose with their Ci Eccles Amethyst in 1972 – another well-known caravanner in this period.

Opposite below: Dame Shirley Bassey poses with her new Lister Salamander caravan in the 1970s.

Caravanning on the canal in 1972. You put your caravan onto a special flatbed boat and went 'cara-sailing'.

diesel engine. The service only lasted a year or two before it was withdrawn, but it was a nice idea. Health and safety wouldn't let it happen today though as it was all too easy to slip into the water if you were not careful.

To summarise as we close this chapter, the first few years of the decade saw so much happening in the world of caravanning. Caravan manufacturers were expanding to keep up with demand, with new factories being built costing thousands of pounds. Orders poured in, especially from abroad. Bailey, Astral, Ace, A-Line and most UK makes had big export orders into Europe. Also, in 1972 Ace Caravans joined static makers Belmont and formed ABI, while Bailey Caravans would be sold by the Bailey family to Winn Industries in 1972 for a £165,000. All was looking good for caravanning in this early part of the decade.

Imported caravans were few and far between, but Tabbert (made in Germany) came to the UK, though they were expensive. Tabberts were well made, solid tourers, but limited numbers saw low sales. Adria would be officially launched at the 1970 Earl's Court Show and signed at least a few dealers up, giving the UK caravanner a Continental choice with a decent spec and being 'different' from their fellow caravanning buddies. Cabby, a name from Sweden, were edging into the UK in 1970, offering a well-built caravan equipped for all-year touring (if you could find a site open). Cabby's party trick was to plant a saloon car on the roof to prove its strength!

Other imports came nearer to home, from Ireland. Pull-Van caravans were luxury models while Freedom was a medium-priced range, along with Rolon. These brands had limited success. The British caravanner knew what they liked and would take some persuading to go 'foreign'.

Above: Imported tourers were few. Tabbert came into the UK by 1970; they were expensive, costing over a £1,000, but well specified.

Below left: Cabby, the Swedish maker, in 1970 used this VW Beetle to demonstrate the strength of their caravan to UK dealers.

Below right: The Irish-made Freedom was imported through Callender Caravans in Lancashire from 1969 to 1971, setting up a small dealer network.

Freedom Caravans 1970

LUXURY RANGE

2

THE OIL CRISIS, INFLATION AND THE THREE-DAY WEEK

As 1972 began to fade, dark clouds were on the horizon for the UK economy. The miners' strike in early 1972 had caused some disruption, but nothing compared to the upset in late 1973. On 1 April 1973 a new tax called VAT was introduced that added 10 per cent to the price of goods and services, which was supposed to be fairer and was aimed at more luxury items. VAT replaced the old purchase tax. It would alter prices of many items that didn't get taxed before. It would increase the cost of caravanning in many ways, including accessories and site fees.

With the news of VAT being added to caravans, manufacturers thought pre-April 1973 would see a boom in sales. Some manufacturers, such as Scottish maker Thomson Caravans, put in magazine ads they were celebrating VAT. There was a surge in overall sales of new tourers, as caravanners upgraded wanted to beat the VAT rise. This then followed with a real levelling-off period in the summer of 1973. 66,000 tourers were produced, but chasing fewer buyers – caravanners decided to keep hold of their current tourer. In this period caravanners were still using caravans from the 1960s; although many wanted to upgrade, they couldn't afford it.

We'd like to help you celebrate v.a.t.

VAT was introduced on 1 April 1973. This Thomson Caravans advert claimed to celebrate this event for a rush in pre-VAT sales.

Oil prices would rise in this period too. Fuel prices increased, with larger cars becoming more expensive to run and inflation climbing to 25 per cent. Caravanners were still venturing further abroad, and it was now more common to spend two weeks abroad with your caravan than ever before. The package holiday had really begun in the late 1960s, with operators such as Thomas Cook making flying to the Continent cheaper. With larger aircraft and more seats, costs were cut and by the mid-1970s a week in Spain didn't cost much and you were also treated to sunshine.

Touring caravans were still viewed as being good value for money, with weekend breaks as well as main holidays catered for. By this era caravans were being fitted with mod cons such as an electric-operated water/foot pump and stainless-steel sink. Medium-priced models offered more too, with 12-volt lighting supplementing gas lights as the main illumination. A new gas light design by Carver was introduced that had spark ignition with a glass fibre shade, which most manufacturers adopted. Cavalier caravans continued with their two model twin axles for tourers and L-shaped kitchen designs. The 490GT 5-metre length was for families. It was £1,684 in 1974 but also came with a high specification, including a fridge and oven.

Right: With better ferry services, caravanners were going abroad in greater numbers than before.

Below: The electric water pump by Whale ran off 12 volts and by the mid-1970s was fitted as standard to mid-priced tourers. By 1973 the new Carver gas light meant there were no more matches or broken glass shades.

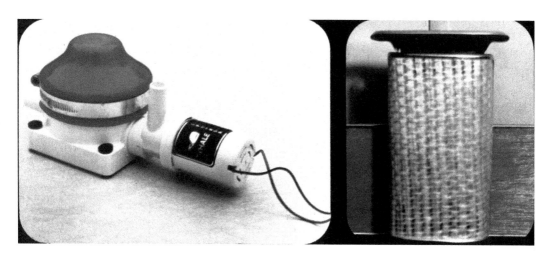

4·90 GTS

16 foot 5 berth

A	6 ft 0 in seat
B	4 ft 0 in seat
E	Bed extension
EE	Shower/toilet extension
ES	Pull-down extension seat
OS	Open shelf
OC	Refrigerator/cooker comp.
OL	Overhead locker
OLC	Overhead locker/cocktail cabinet
P	Pullman bunk
R	Roof locker
S	Sink unit
STC	Shower/toilet compartment
SD	Sliding divider
T	Table
TC	Toilet compartment
W	Wardrobe
WH	Water heater
OW	Opening window
FW	Fixed window

Specification

Body length	16 ft 0 in
Overall length	19 ft 6 in
Internal width	6 ft 4¾ in
Overall width	6 ft 8½ in
Maximum headroom	6 ft 1¼ in
Overall height	8 ft 3½ in
No. of berths	Five
Tyres	5·20×13 4 ply
Tyre pressure	30 lb psi
Ex works weight	19·75 cwt
Ex works nose weight	130 lb
Maximum gross weight	23·6 cwt
2 cu ft R.A.M. 24 gas refrigerator	

Cavalier Caravans made a success of their twin-axle tourers from 1972. The 74 GTS came with a fridge and water heater as standard – the kitchen was a selling feature.

In 1970 Bailey Caravans launched their first twin-axle model: the Mikouri, costing £1,264 in 1974, which was designed for touring and was 5.80 metres in length. Limited in sales, Bailey built it until 1975. Few cars were big enough to tow a tourer this size unless you bought something like a Land Rover. Prices on caravans were increasing; for instance, a 1972 Sprite Alpine cost £438, but by September 1973 it had risen to £559 – a substantial increase back then. To combat this rise in prices manufacturers tried to improve the specifications, so buyers could at least see they were getting a little more for the price increase. But luxury makes now had models over a £1,000.

In late 1971 the *Glass's Guide* for caravans and statics was published for the first time. With dealer research, the guide gave a good indication to market prices. For trade only, close ties with manufacturers kept the guide up to date on new models and makers. Published every quarter, the guide gave useful insights to the state of the market and what models caravanners were buying on the used forecourts.

By 1973 the towing limit was at last raised from 40 to 50 mph after several years of discussions. Caravanners had to display a 50-mph sticker on the caravan's rear panel, while displaying the weight of tow vehicle and caravan, with the latter not exceeding the car's kerb weight. My dad was keen to place a 50-mph sticker on the Welton's rear panel and display the weights. It didn't stop Dad from being pulled towing at 55 mph by a patrol car, though he was let off.

GLASS'S GUIDE
CARAVAN VALUES
TOWED . RESIDENTIAL

SEPTEMBER 1971
PUBLISHED QUARTERLY
NEXT ISSUE . 1st DECEMBER 1971

Right: The *Glasses Guide* was the salesman's Bible. This first 1971 edition was followed each quarter.

Below: The 50-mph towing limit brought into force in 1973 meant new regulations had to be adhered to meet the requirements.

In this period caravanners could still ask a farmer for a spot for a few nights on his land. For a loo the caravanner was asked to dig his own trench, around 30 cm deep, and then dig another hole and fill it with stones to act as a soak-away for waste water. This practice was rare by this time, but possible. Caravanning was changing as new larger parks installed bars, cafés, kids' entertainment areas and swimming pools – usually outside. Larger site operating groups invested more heavily, attracting more into taking up caravanning.

At the back end of 1972, after months of talks with dealers, Sam Alper's Ci Group changed their retail policy to solus trading. Ci's touring brands – Sprite, Europa, Eccles and Fairholme – complete with a spares back up and support were only to be stocked, with the exception of a hand-built luxury manufacturer such as Safari or Carlight luxury caravan brands. Some dealerships welcomed the Ci-only idea, with financial support and premises painted to Ci colour schemes with full factory training for repair work. Other dealers, such as the then large Gailey retail group, saw it as Ci's way of dominating the market and dropped the Ci brands.

Alper's idea was to give Ci buyers top service and well-managed dealerships, adding a more professional approach to caravan retail. Ci had twenty-nine models across their ranges, so caravan buyers had a good choice in layouts and specifications. ABI launched its answer with the budget range Monza, aiming to put them into Spriteless dealerships. Caravanners who had tight budgets yet wanted a good, lightweight, value caravan now had the Monza range, which offered a choice over Sprite, and a good one at that. ABI would buy Elddis Caravans in 1973, strengthening ABI's market growth while adding new ranges

In the 1970s outdoor swimming pools on larger sites were popular, especially on a decent summer's day. (Photo courtesy of Holgate Group)

Above: Ci dealers could take one luxury non-competing brand on, such as luxury hand-built Carlight tourers.

Right: The Monza 1000 met the Ci Sprite 400 head-on in size, price and finish. The 1974 Monza was £516 to the 400's £488.

such as Target and Ace Awards. The caravanner of the 1970s had plenty of new models to look at.

In late 1973 oil-producing countries (OPEC) cut back on oil production. This caused a shock to the West as prices rocketed. With UK industrial unrest, the country's coal miners voted for an overtime ban, cutting production so much that the coal-fired power stations had to cut output. Power cuts were introduced while petrol prices increased along with raw material prices. There were petrol shortages and I remember Dad getting a petrol ration book in the post, which wasn't ever needed in the end. Even so, a 50-mph national speed limit was made law on 8 December 1973 to cut down the consumption of fuel – surprisingly, no law was actioned to stop caravan towing. The 70-mph limit returned later in March 1974 on motorways and by May on other roads. The petrol shortage caused major problems for larger-engined cars, with sales slumping and affecting resale values.

With the three-day working week due to the energy crisis, caravan production was hit. With surplus 1973 models being discounted, this was ideal for those buyers who could afford a new tourer. With rising costs and inflation, the following year's new 1974 models had risen in cost by as much as 15 per cent, slowing sales as new caravan buyers stalled. Just 25,000 tourers in 1974 were produced, with several caravan manufacturers cutting drastically back. Not since the war days had caravanning been hit so hard, with even long-established names such as Cheltenham Caravans closing down.

With cost rising and the Sprite/Monza budget sector still selling steadily, other established caravan makers also entered this cheaper-end sector to help their general sales. Names that entered the lower end of the market included Piper by Abbey, Excel by Forest, Prima by Bailey, Perle by Avondale, Clan by Thomson, Sprint by Ci, Lyncraft by Lynton, Kestrel by Fleetwind, and Scout by Astral. All these names were scrambling for new sales in the entry-level sector to keep the factories flowing. To keep costs and weight down the

After VAT hit, sales dropped. And the over production of seventy-three models meant discounts for caravanners wanting a bargain.

The demise of the clubman hand-built tourer, such as Cheltenham by the mid-1970s, was to see others fall by the next decade.

designs of the above were simple and low spec. Ci's Sprite market was under attack. As a caravanner wanting a new low cost tourer you now had so much more choice.

Although the holiday package market had been doing well it also began to suffer with higher costs, just as caravanning had – no leisure pursuit could escape the rising costs. Some manufacturers would shut down while the bigger companies had stocks of new, unsold caravans in fields. The small dealerships would suffer as the three-day week came in on 31 December 1973. Some would stop trading, but others struggled through. A gallon of petrol now cost 50p in 1974 (90p by 1979), making towing more costly. 1974 saw costs skyrocket as the cost of living was rising too; my parents complained about how much electric had gone up, and food too.

Mini car sales increased and a few caravan makers designed small caravans towable by the Mini. Victor Caravans of Batley (part of the Kenmore Caravans dealership) thought they had the answer with the Mini Victor, but by the end of 1974 they had stopped manufacturing them. Thomson had their Mini Glen, another tiny tourer that was a steady seller. And Ci had its lightweight three-berth Cadet Mk 2.

Turning to advances in caravanning, one major step forward was the new auto-reverse system that was introduced by big UK caravan chassis manufacturer B&B Trailers in September 1973. The Sigma hitch allowed the caravanner to reverse without leaving the car to manually throw the catch to stop the overrun brakes being activated. This new

With the fuel crisis several small tourers hit the market. In 1974, Victor Caravans launched its Mini models designed for Mini car owners.

innovation meant that UK caravanners needed to learn to reverse – a tricky operation for most. Although several electronic devices to aid reversing were tried, the Sigma design was the benchmark. Caravan chassis were spray painted when manufactured and many caravanners had a winter/spring job repainting the chassis to hold back rusting.

Some caravan dealers would offer this repaint service; others would spray the chassis with oil for protection instead. The coupling and corner steadies would need a going over with a grease gun while the brakes were adjusted. Caravan servicing wasn't carried out on a regular basis as it is in modern times, and that was mainly because there was little equipment. I remember Dad and his friend doing jobs on their caravans, with Dad donning his old clothes and spending the afternoon underneath with a wire brush, then using rust-resistant paint to protect the chassis. DIY caravan jobs were still in vogue and winter months saw a caravan owner on stepladders resealing the seams or adding a TV aerial bracket or awning rail.

The five van sites or CLs that the Caravan Club had brought in had by this time reached over 3,000. These sites had grown in popularity and my parents would often use these mainly basic farm sites opposed to larger concerns. Some of these CLs were in large front gardens and adult only, while others were on private grounds. I can't really remember going on what I would call a large site, apart from a few; my parents liked smaller sites with no bars or pool.

Chassis needed painting every few years. In early September 1973, UK main chassis supplier B&B Trailers launched the Sigma auto-reverse hitch.

Caravanning began to slowly recover, but a move in 1975 by the government increased VAT on luxury items to 25 per cent. Touring caravans came under this and prices shot up again. The NCC organised a lobby to Parliament, with several outfits doing a circular tour with posters stuck on the caravans and slogans against the extra VAT on touring caravans. The following year the higher VAT was taken off tourers and reduced to 10 per cent, though used caravans had sold well in 1975 creating a used shortage while new models hardly moved.

In 1974 the Ci Group placed a 30-second Sprite advert on national TV – a first by any caravan manufacturer. It not only brought the Ci Sprite brand into people's living rooms, but also caravanning itself. The advert launched in early January of that year. It was expensive but gave reasonable results. Ci would also sponsor the European Sports Car Championship – again, a new idea by a caravan manufacturer. The car was a Lola 300-bhp car driven by Guy Edwards for the 1975 season. The car had all the Ci logos on it and was a way of promoting the brand with TV coverage thrown in for free.

In this era entry-level caravans were more affordable for new caravanners, so Ci used their production expertise to produce a new super entry-level lightweight tourer – the Ci Sprint. Costing £756 in 1975, at 3.90 metres in length it slept four or five and was light enough (431 kgs unladen) to be towed by the Mini car. It offered a cheap new tourer, which, while very basic, was easy to upgrade if needed. In this era caravanners would still fit their own water pumps, fridges and ovens. The Ci Sprint would prove a reasonable success, with a 4.26-metre model being added for 1976. New caravanners wanted an affordable lightweight caravan, while these entry-level caravans kept dealership sales relatively buoyant.

Left: NCC car and caravan protest in 1975 outside Parliament to scrap the increased 25 per cent VAT on new caravans that was hurting caravanners' pockets.

Below: Ci Group sponsored the Sports Car Championship in 1975, with the Lola 300 BHP car giving Ci a high profile.

Caravan heating was to improve further in the mid-1970s. An innovative design of heating for hardy winter caravanners would be the wet heating system by the Swedish company Primus. The Primus boiler was placed in the front gas locker and once running it would heat up with a thermostat control, sending heat around the caravan. The hot water system was also operated from the Primus system. It worked on gas only, but also could be used with mains electrics if

The Ci Sprint 12 was cheap and cheerful. It was launched to bolster poor sales in 1975.

a site had a mains supply. The Primus wet heating system was fitted to a few UK luxury tourers, but weight and cost was a factor in sales and popularity.

Also in 1974/5, Swedish firm Alde was to launch into the UK. It offered a lighter weight system, but a cost of £300 was not a selling point for UK buyers and Primus would have the better success. Alde disappeared from the UK for some years, but was used by Ci in their high-spec Europa 455, built for the Swedish market in 1978. Alde would also have a connection for mains operation and unusually offered the system for static caravans too.

KEEP WARM!

Hot water for the sink

CENTRAL HEATING

Thermostat for easy heat control

Primus heat exchanger on A-frame

Hot water for wash basin

Heat from the convectors

Primus Swedish's wet heating system had appeared in the UK from 1974/75 – the boiler was housed in the front gas locker.

Most UK caravanners went for the gas Carver convector heater, which could be added with a 12-volt-run fan for blown air. My parents had their existing Carver SB1800 heater converted to do this, with a blown outlet fitted in the lounge area of their Welton.

In this period the Ci Group celebrated its Sprite brand in 1973 with a special edition Alpine C model – then still the UK's bestselling caravan. With extras added such as carpet, a foot pump, 12-volt lighting, special paint and graphics, this van was put into production, with around 133 built as a limited edition. Sprite had begun to lose its lead by the late 1970s as other brands became established in its market sector – none more so than the ABI Monza.

Around the mid-1970s there were several books for the caravanner with useful tips for beginners and experienced caravanners too. For a few years Sells Books published a new caravan buyer's guide. These were excellent at the time and had all the latest makes with layouts and cost. I bought the 1974 issue from my local WHSmith with my pocket money.

One book that provided a factual, historic account of the caravan industry and caravanning was *The History of the Caravan* by Bill Whiteman (Blandford Press, 1973). Whitman, who had been around from the early days of caravanning, knew many pioneers of the caravanning movement and was a keen caravanner himself. He had vast knowledge of caravans and had been the editor of *Caravan Magazine* from the 1930s and helped to form the National Caravan Council. In that period, he was the industry's voice.

Needless to say, some birthday cash and pocket money converted into a postal order. Payment was sent direct to the publisher and a week later it arrived. This brilliant book also covered motorhomes as well as park homes and holiday caravans. If you're lucky, the odd one still comes up for sale in used bookshops.

In the next chapter we look at accessories and a few other things that were going on in the world of caravanning in this decade.

TREAT YOURSELF TO A LITTLE LUXURY...

Treat yourself to just a little luxury in your own caravan, holiday home or residential with the famous Swedish Alde-Verken central heating system.

For a modest outlay, you can have central heating with hot and cold running water facility installed in your present caravan. And for the man who goes abroad each year, there's the option of a special plug-in mains for Continental camping sites.

The Alde-Verken system has many winning features that have made it the most popular and successful central heating installation for caravans in the cold climates of Sweden.

Prices start at approximately £300 including installation in your own caravan, holiday home or residential. Send stamp to your nearest installation agents for more details:

The Alde-Verken wet heating system was launched in the UK by 1975 and cost an expensive £300 to be fitted to most tourers.

SELL'S GUIDE TO TOURING

CARAVANS

60p

THE CARAVAN BUYERS GUIDE 1974

Above: Caravanners could check out the latest tourers of that year with the *Sell's Guide to Touring Caravans*. I bought this copy from WHSmith in 1974.

Right: Bill Whitman's *The History of the Caravan* was a fascinating book for caravanners wanting to learn about their pastime's heritage.

W. M. WHITEMAN

THE HISTORY OF THE CARAVAN

3

CARAVAN ACCESSORIES AND A RIGHT CARRY ON!

Although we have covered some accessories already, we will have a look at a few more in this short chapter and also take a brief look into caravans on the big screen. I have talked about tow cars and what the most popular ones of the decade were. Of course, they all had petrol engines unless you towed with a diesel Land Rover. But manual gearboxes were the general trend in this period. The advantages of towing with an auto box were many; however, because they had extra strain, towing could cause the box to over heat. So, all automatic cars needed an oil cooler fitted as an option – very few had one as standard. Diesel cars would begin to appear too, though later in the decade, gaining more popularity by the 1980s.

When it came to caravanning accessories, most dealerships would stock plenty of varied kinds. Even small dealers catered for caravanners buying essential bits. From water carriers and Calor gas to other caravanning items such as sleeping bags, loos and security devices. Other accessories included towing mirrors, which were available in various types of design. There were 12-volt strip lights to ovens, heaters and front covers to stop your caravan front getting stone chipped – seems nothing's new! With more 12-volt-powered items caravanners would carry another car battery. Usually this was in a bed locker, so caravan manufacturers began making the front gas lockers larger with a place for a battery – not an idea that would be allowed today. You charged it on the move using the car's alternator to top it up.

The accessory market grew with such ideas as a caravan step manufactured from tough plastic instead of wood or metal, which were the norm in the 1970s. Water pumps by Whale and Jupiter, operated by foot or hand, pumped the water from the container outside to the kitchen sink, though Whale did make a 12-volt (GP73) electric model that caravan manufacturers began fitting as standard by the mid-1970s. The Aquaroll brand water container had been around since the 1950s, but by the 1970s onwards it would become the caravanner's main choice. By the start of the 1970s they were manufactured with plastic, replacing the aluminium – the cost was £6.15 in 1972.

Then there was the Porta Shower. Now, some upmarket caravan makers put this in as standard, but you could buy it from around £8 in 1972. You filled it with warm water then primed it and then you had a shower of sorts.

Then there were winches. We had to store our caravan behind my grandparent's bungalow, which involved getting it up a steep slope. A winch designed especially for

Above: Most caravan dealerships, no matter how small, had a shop with accessories stocked, though smaller dealers usually just had the basic essentials.

Right: To help with bad stone dents caravanners could buy a canvas front cover, which tied to the grab handles.

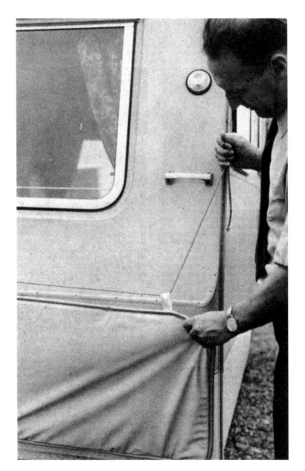

caravanners with that problem was available. It was quite a long-winded operation, but it did solve the problem for many.

There was also the easy coupler. If your car couldn't get close to couple up to the caravan because of soft ground then you winched it over to the tow car. The manufacturers used the comment 'The wife can do it' to advertise its simplicity, which was demeaning and sexist, but this was the 1970s.

Above: The porta-shower for the 1970s caravanner – I doubt if many were sold over the decade.

Below: The miniwinch offered help to the caravanner pulling up gradients – Dad even considered one.

Then there was the easy coupler – a typical caravanner's aid to hitching up. The phrase in the ad, 'the wife can do it', is very 1970s.

There were display areas for awnings and such things as tables, chairs and BBQs. Cup and saucer sets emerged especially for the caravanner – usually light and durable. There were water containers of various forms and also caravan loos. This market saw caravan loo manufacturers produce designs offering things better than the other on flushing, emptying and even the liquid used in them. Then there was clothing designed for the caravanner, with boots and waterproof leggings, hats and gloves. These now look comical in modern times, but wet long grass was no joy and wet sites would also see cars getting stuck in mud. You could buy grip mats from your dealer's shop to put under the car's drive wheels to help in these situations. Or the caravan ski, which fitted under the jockey wheel so you could slide it over boggy or muddy ground.

Fridges were popular, with caravanners ordering a fridge with a new caravan, and a heater too as already mentioned. There were lots of towing mirrors available. Dad had a Raydyot clip-on, which fitted over the front wing mirror – remember wing mirrors? Or you could have a Stadium brand clamp-on mirror, but what about the 1970s paintwork? Chocks for levelling your caravan on an uneven pitch were a must, though Dad's friend made him some from spare wood as you did back then. In *Practical Caravan* there was 'how to' guides, such as fitting a water pump, hand basin in a loo compartment and other various DIY jobs. Although caravan theft was relatively rare you could invest in a hitch lock, which fitted the ball coupling then had a padlock. Looking back, Dad had one, but I reckon a child could have picked it! Other locks and battery-run alarms were marketed but I can't remember anybody my parents caravanned with having anything fitted to deter a thief.

The 1970s caravanner had a growing assortment of accessories with plastic cups, flasks, dishes and a clip-on table storage basket.

Don't laugh! This lady wearing protective rainwear is off to fill her kettle up. This attire was typical of this period in caravanning.

There were plenty of towing mirrors available. For £2 you could have this Stadium-branded clamp-on mirror. Stadium also made motorbike helmets.

One of the most popular accessories being fitted was the 12-volt strip light. Some caravanners began using these instead of the gas lights. Better and more efficient designs saw this market expand and caravanners wanted more 12-volt lighting in their caravans. By 1983 gas lighting would be phased out in new tourers. Lab Craft were leaders in this field, manufacturing charger units and control panels as well as strip lighting. Radios and cassette players were another new 1970s accessory, fit for those who took their music seriously. Caravanners who had children fitted made-to-measure covers to keep the originals protected – several companies offered this service. By the end of this decade, though, fewer caravanners used made-to-measure covers, using throw overs instead.

Mesh fly screens were sometimes added by caravanners, and even a form of poor retro-fit double glazing using Perspex sheets. To charge a separate caravan battery, site owners provided this service for the cost of 20p, or you could buy a portable wind generator. In the mid- to late 1970s Kawasaki and Honda would create new smaller and quieter portable petrol generators. Mainly used by boating folk, caravanners who wanted to run a TV off the mains and charge a separate battery also found a generator useful. Site owners though would in many cases put in rules of how long a generator could be left to run. It wasn't uncommon for fellow caravanners to complain about a petrol generator being left on all night. In this period demand due to the power cuts meant getting one was also difficult.

With fuel costs climbing, ideas to cut the cost of towing came into being. Firstly, the car roof-mounted airfoil was introduced, one being named 'The Wind Slammer'. But you had to experiment to get the best results and many thought it created more drag. Some users

illuminating facts from Lab·Craft about the all·electric caravan!

This is the age of the all–electric caravan. Are you missing out by condemning yourself now to a gloomy procession of dull evenings?

Why be in the dark about the simple facts of conversion, when filling in and mailing the coupon below can throw a whole new ght on the subject.

Whether permanently sited or used for touring, Lab-Craft products open up a bright new world for you. And at very reasonable cost.

12 volt battery operated units by Lab-Craft, pioneers in miniature lighting. Fitted by many leading caravan manufacturers as Original Equipment.

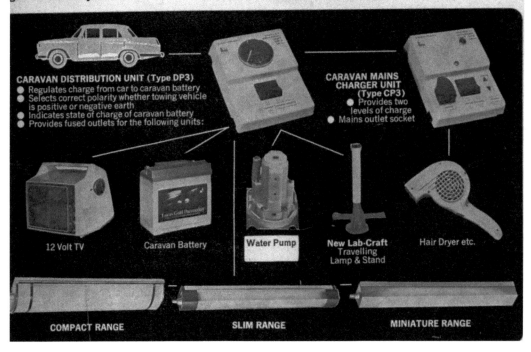

CARAVAN DISTRIBUTION UNIT (Type DP3)
● Regulates charge from car to caravan battery
● Selects correct polarity whether towing vehicle is positive or negative earth
● Indicates state of charge of caravan battery
● Provides fused outlets for the following units:

CARAVAN MAINS CHARGER UNIT (Type CP3)
● Provides two levels of charge
● Mains outlet socket

12 Volt TV   Caravan Battery   Water Pump   New Lab-Craft Travelling Lamp & Stand   Hair Dryer etc.

COMPACT RANGE   SLIM RANGE   MINIATURE RANGE

Lab-craft were innovators in caravan 12-volt lighting and dominated the market from the mid-1970s.

were convinced they got better fuel results. They were often seen in the mid- to late 1970s, with some caravanners using the aerofoil to put stickers of places they'd visited on. Or you could buy an inflatable front type nose cone that was tied to the front of the caravan – it didn't catch on.

With fuel costs, towing your tourer cost more than ever. These roof-mounted aerofoils convinced many to buy one for lower fuel consumption while towing.

By 1975/6 you could buy a portable colour TV. Panasonic were one of the first to introduce them. It ran off battery and mains, but was designed to cut out before it drained the battery. The cost was around £200! By this period sleeping bags had improved and more choice of grade warmth had become available, with Polywarm being a top UK brand.

One item you could not buy from your dealership shop was the special Rally shower-proof lightweight jacket from *Caravan Magazine* for £3.20. For Christmas 1973 I received one complete with a *Caravan Magazine* woven badge. It was one of my best presents. I thought how cool I looked and wore it at any opportunity. I had that jacket for many years.

Caravanning was to get some media coverage in the mid-1970s. The sitcom *Whatever Happened to the Likely Lads?* had a spin-off film in 1976. Our two lads took a Sprite Alpine on holiday with Bob's wife and Terry's girlfriend. Shot in and around Northumberland, the Alpine ends up getting rammed by Bob driving the tow car into the Sprite's back end.

Caravans also featured alongside the *Carry On* team in the film aptly named *Carry On Behind* released in 1976. The film set on a caravan site with various characters in their caravans ends up in typical *Carry On* style. All the caravans supplied were Ci brands – Sprite, Eccles, Europa and Fairholme. The film was shot in March and was portrayed as being in the height of summer. It's a typical 1970s film full of non-PC scenes but laughable all the same. Films like these did give caravanning greater exposure and it was typical of Sam Alper to grab the limelight, with his Ci brands supplying models. *Carry On Behind* is a regular repeat on TV.

Despite the lows in the economy and the energy crisis, caravanning survived. And with new accessories to make the hobby more comfortable and homelike, it still attracted new blood. Caravanning was changing and with caravanners wanting more home comforts, even basic caravans began to see items fitted as standard that were once extra just a few years before. The end of the 2970s saw greater changes and challenges as cost and more competition from other holiday forms threatens caravanning's popularity.

One third of your holiday you'll spend asleep. Spend it in 'Polywarm' comfort.

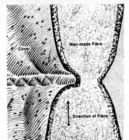

There were several brands of sleeping bags, but Polywarm were regarded as the best.

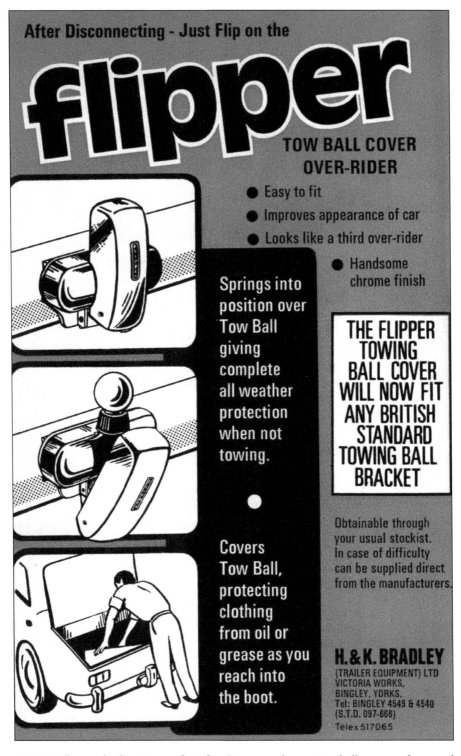
H. K. Bradley made chassis parts but also this super chrome tow ball cover aptly named Flipper. I remember this cover being popular especially on Rovers and Jags of the time.

The author on
Bispham Beach
in 1975 wearing
what I thought was
cool: my *Caravan
Magazine* jacket.
Did it woo the girls?
Well, no!

Be Exclusive

a caravan rally jacket for £3.20 post free

Exclusive to readers of CARAVAN we offer these lightweight showerproof nylon rally jackets, as worn by the CARAVAN team on the British Caravan Road Rally. Exclusively tailored with hard-wearing zip, knitted cuffs and mandarin collar these durable jackets can be sponged clean. Large side pocket and handy sleeve pocket. In red with white stripes and available in three sizes.

PLUS
superior-quality woven CARAVAN cloth badge, exclusive to our readers.

caravan price

£3.20 State size—small (36-38), medium (38-40), large (40-42)

Send cheques or postal orders to Caravan Jackets Offer, Link House, Dingwall Avenue, Croydon CR9 2TA. Allow up to three weeks for delivery.

Caravan Magazine's
special 'Caravan
Road Rally Jacket'
was a reader offer in
late 1973/74 – Mum
ordered me one for
Christmas.

Carry On Behind released in 1976. A press shot shows Windsor Davies (right) and Jack Douglas (left) outside a Ci Europa on set.

4

CARAVANNING AT THE END OF THE DECADE

The hot summer of 1976 saw sites booked up as caravanners made the most of the dry weather. Caravanners had witnessed a number of caravan brands that had gone to the wall over the last few years, but at the latter end of the decade a few new names made their debut. In this period the caravanner was never short on choices. With tougher trading in 1975 smaller dealerships would suffer, many shutting as the bigger ones took more market share. Gone were the days of many dealers covering the same area.

Caravanners would travel to get the better deal, especially with improved road networks, and this was emphasised with the Earl's Court show where dealers were getting keener to clinch that deal. The caravan buyer had more power in the bargaining arena as dealers undercut one another. The London show was still seen as the show to visit, especially for a deal, but distance for warranty work wasn't always taken into consideration when buying from a dealership a couple of hundred miles away. That deal at times would turn out a nightmare when things went wrong! There were local dealer shows set up and many of them grew well, including the February Birmingham Bingley Hall show, which had gotten so big it moved to the new NEC building by 1977. Other shows in Glasgow and Manchester were operating too – again, at the start of the new year and dealer run.

New caravan construction ideas were being implemented at this time. Dormobile resurfaced into caravan manufacturing for the UK market from 1976 with their all-season caravans featuring bonded one-piece aluminium seamless sides and double-glazed plastic windows. Dormobile used adhesives to fix sides to the chassis framework instead of bolting the sides on. The Dormobile's body framework was steel with minimum wood used, which was unusual at the time. The Dormobile tourer was advanced for this period, using construction ideas that are used today and hailed as a new innovation!

These new ideas were designed to offer caravanners a caravan that would be more durable with extra specifications, which caravanners in the late 1970s were expecting. Ex-Bailey sales manger David Rose founded his caravan manufacturing firm Monolite. In 1976, Rose gave his tourers one-piece aluminium sides with no joins, cutting down the risk of leaks – again, this is something we see in modern caravans. With a fully bonded and fully insulated body, Rose's caravans met with a problem manufacturing so he had

The Earl's Court Caravan Show was a big event in caravanning if you wanted to see the latest in caravans and accessories.

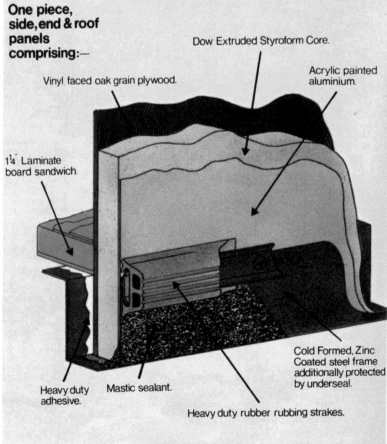

One piece, side, end & roof panels comprising:—

Dow Extruded Styroform Core.

Vinyl faced oak grain plywood.

Acrylic painted aluminium.

$1\frac{1}{4}''$ Laminate board sandwich.

Cold Formed, Zinc Coated steel frame additionally protected by underseal.

Heavy duty adhesive.

Mastic sealant.

Heavy duty rubber rubbing strakes.

Dormobile caravans had far-thinking ideas in caravan construction, using adhesives and steel framework cutting out wood.

Dormobile were famous for motorhomes and campervans, but their later models (pictured) in 1976 met with some success.

to design a special press for this operation to be carried out. Caravanners didn't like the white, plain sides – they were used to trim where panel joints met. So, he attached these for aesthetic purposes to please buyers and break up the panel.

The Monolites were built on a lightweight aluminium chassis, and lighting was by 12-volt strip lights. Rose also fitted new Contora brand tinted double-glazed plastic windows too. The profiles were simple, but weight saved meant a Ford Cortina 1.3 could tow their 1977 Challenger 4.5-metre berth with relative ease. Caravanning was entering a new stage.

Mains electrics were added on some large parks, where the electrics were often metered to charge based on usage. There weren't any real set standards on caravan plug-in mains electrics, but this would change by the early 1980s.

Sites were better planned than ever, with more facilities being added. Caravanners wanted improved pitches and toilets with clean shower blocks. The late 1970s were seeing changes and by 1977 my parents had reluctantly sold the Welton for a new Elddis Tornado. This was swapped in the summer for another Elddis, a Mistral limited edition Silver Jubilee made to celebrate the Queen's twenty-five years. Being a two-berth, my caravanning was limited to day visits now. It was one of, I think, thirty-seven jubilee editions made. The Queen's Silver Jubilee saw street parties and parades, and caravan sites also had their own celebrations.

Dad had now become the owner of a British Leyland Princess 2200 wedge design. It was ideal, Dad said, for towing with its smooth six-cylinder engine. I could also do front wheel spins with it, but I obviously didn't tell him that! In this period the motorhome and

Above: The Queen's Silver Jubilee in 1977 saw parties and parades. This person is towing a 1977 Fisher Petite behind his tricycle in Staining, Lancashire. (Photo courtesy of Audrey Bendall)

Below: Some caravanners also towed with a campervan or motorhome. Here is a VW-based unit with a 1974 Elddis Tornado – note the lady's flared trousers.

campervan had also seen a rise in sales, only slowing with the fuel crisis. Some caravanners would change over to a motorhome, which was helped by improved chassis cabs from Ford, Bedford and Commer. But in some cases caravanners bought a campervan and had the best of both worlds towing the caravan with it.

Astral, a big Hull caravan maker, launched their new Shadow line-up. These were basically export models but were added to the UK Astral line-up. On the Shadow they used the German chassis maker Al-Ko, which was galvanised. This meant no more painting and also a less complicated, lighter design, yet still very strong. Astral would be the only big UK manufacturer to use the Al-Ko chassis, but other tourer manufacturers would follow in the next decade.

Autosport Caravans, a dealership at Bicester owned by Eric Prue, who had been involved with the Caravan Road Rally event, had designed a new super aerodynamic tourer. Prue built his new caravan on the new Al-Ko chassis, setting the wheels slightly further back for increased stability. The Alpha 14 was launched as a family and couples layout. Its profile wasn't to caravanners' tastes, however, and build quality wasn't the best. Around eighty were made from 1977 to 1981. Caravanners wanted a practically designed caravan, which the Alpha wasn't.

Caravanning was a popular family holiday break and, with the car market changing, by 1976 a new sector appeared between a small and medium saloon/estate – a new breed of caravanner was on their way. Families with a smaller car who still wanted to go caravanning could, by 1977, do so with the newly launched Ford Fiesta.

The Alpha caravan was great on tow. Its axle was placed further back than normal. An Al-Ko chassis was used but the quality wasn't the best.

Sprite Aerial (3.02 metres) replaced the 400 in early 1976, but for Fiesta owners with the 1.1 engine the Sprite was ideal for young families on a budget.

This new breed of cars was known as a hatchback. They were cars that offered economy yet was still able to take the two kids and granny too if needed. The traditional 3.5-metre-length family tourer with a rear dinette, centre kitchen with wardrobe opposite and a single-width settee or single dinette with a bunk above was a layout that was disappearing from medium-priced caravans. Making the body slightly longer meant that a small loo compartment could be added by moving the layout around. This layout would win out in the end, with the added loo compartment meaning no dashing to the site toilets during the night.

Though not as popular, the 3.5-metre-length layout was used for cheaper, lightweight models such as the 1979 Ci Cadet 10 and the A-Line Imp, which was almost a clone of the Cadet. Both were designed for the new cars such as the VW Golf, Ford Fiesta, Vauxhall Chevette and Renault 5. Fisher Caravans, an old maker, made some interesting small caravans. In late 1976 they launched the Petite 260 with rear door entry – very much in the same vein as the Sprite Cadet Mk 1 from 1970. The Fisher was a wedge shape mainly due to the construction.

Bonded sides used an aluminium frame, which the side panels slotted in and were then screwed to each other at the corners. This happened to the roof too, which again used the aluminium supporting frames to attach and screw the roof on. Light in weight, this wedge-shaped tiny Fisher tourer was towed by Sterling Moss with a Vespa scooter at the Goodwood Motorama event as a PR stunt. Although sales were reasonable, they didn't sell in great numbers.

It was in this period that caravanners were expecting more for their money. Items such as fridges were being fitted on medium-priced tourers, which now ran off the 12-volt

Right: By stretching the body to 3.2 metres a tiny room for a toilet could be included, such as with this 1978 A-Line Rambler budget model.

Below: The Ci Cadet was a 3.02-metre-long budget lightweight, which cost £1,079 when launched in 1979.

A-Line Caravans' new Imp was a clone of the CI Cadet 10. This PR shot shows individual dealers taking one back to their dealership from the factory in convoy.

Stirling Moss on a Vespa towing the new advanced lightweight Fisher 260, proving how easy it was to tow – note no helmet was worn.

system while the caravan was towed. The idea was that because the internal 12-volt lights were on caravans, this also increased the compulsory fitting of fog lights on caravans. From 1 October 1979 a separate electrics plug was to be added. Known as the 'grey socket', the new socket was wired and separate from the road lights. So if you wanted to use the 12-volt power for lighting you could buy an extension lead that had a grey plug on it and went into the car. On the reel you had another grey plug that you attached the caravan's grey plug into.

The boom in caravanning began to wane as the decade progressed. Production figures showed fluctuations with economic circumstances and competition from other holiday styles. Production figures of touring caravans showed demand with highs and lows: 1970 – 36,300; 1971 – 35,500; 1972 – 67,000; 1973 – 66,000; 1974 – 25,000; 1975 – 28,000; 1976 – 36,244; 1977 – 42,451; 1978 – 38,521; and 1979 – 37,568. The numbers were a roller coaster. Those heady days had gone but also there were a lot of caravans in circulation, so it was still popular but perhaps not as buoyant as previous years.

In December 1977 a law was implemented that all new touring caravans would need to have toughened glass or use plastic windows. This meant that by 1978/9 on more expensive ranges most manufacturers would swap over to plastic and also be double glazed. Plastic was lighter in weight but, as many caravanners found out, they scratched easily if not cleaned with care. However, the plastic windows used made glass window caravans look dated.

In this decade a new historic caravan movement was set up to preserve caravanning's heritage. From the 1920s caravans were rescued from fields and restored. Harold Catt was the

By 1979 the new twin light socket was brought in, so a separate plug could run the new compulsory rear fog light plus the interior lights and fridge on tow.

● *Mr. D. M. Brown with his 1922 Rover/1925 Eccles outfit*

The Historic Caravan Register was set up in this decade to help preserve caravans from a bygone age. Two clubs do this today – the Historic Caravan Club and Period & Classic Caravan Club.

main person behind this new movement, saving some from the scrap heap. It later became the Historic Caravan Register and then the Historic Caravan Club, which is still going today.

The Ci Group were also trying to continue bringing caravanners who bought their new Ci tourers a professional service, in line with car manufacturers. They announced their Supercare Parts and Service centres at Ci dealerships. The new service meant Ci could ensure supplying parts faster, even for older Ci Group tourers, along with extended warranties to give confidence to caravan buyers. The idea proved successful. Your supplying Ci dealer could look up parts on the new Ci microfilm parts system and order direct if the dealer didn't hold the stock. Then there was the Ci finance scheme, launched to allow buyers to spread the cost of purchasing a new Ci tourer. No other caravan manufacturer offered such a service, proving again Ci's future vision of more satisfied caravanners.

Towing a caravan was a scary experience for many, while others took to it like a duck to water. In the latter part of the decade towing centres were being set up with courses on safe caravan towing. There were courses that actually took you through chassis design and how the braking system worked on a caravan. A weekend course would cost around £11 in 1978. Pupils were shown how to hitch and unhitch a caravan safely, along with reversing, motorway towing, how to avoid snaking and how to load the caravan correctly. Ci loaned caravans for the summer-run courses, though just a handful of these course were in operation. It was hoped that by 1979 there would be a nationwide caravan-towing training scheme, but this never materialised. The few available courses were often booked up in advance. Those who attended received a certificate to verify their new towing skills.

Right: By the late 1970s Ci had their own finance set up for buyers of new Ci tourers. It also helped Ci secure sales.

Below: By 1978, towing courses were being set up, with larger concerns having new Ci tourers on loan. These courses were quite comprehensive.

Put yourself in the picture...
with **Ci** FINANCE

It helps you to have your caravan NOW...before the inevitable price increases.

A worthwhile possession giving you care-free, money saving holidays year after year.

It is the right type of finance for caravans.

See your Ci Dealer.

Ci FINANCE is a company jointly operated by Caravans International Limited and Industrial Bank of Scotland Limited

Although caravanners generally had a good choice of caravan styles, by the mid-1970s the imported market had begun to take off with makers such as Fendt, Hobby, LMC, Burnster, Cabby, Polar, Tabbert, Knaus, Dethleffs and Polish, which made tourer named Preedom. The imported market was niche but Yugoslavian maker Adria had paved the way in the UK for others.

Interestingly, the caravan king Sam Alper was asked in 1979 to predict how he thought caravan design would change for 2005. Alper spoke of more style in caravans, including larger window areas and sunroofs. He also predicted that construction would use less wood and lighter materials with better insulation qualities. Alper also predicted caravan manufacturers would be fewer, but these would be larger concerns, and that caravan design and manufacture would become more complex as he saw the greater use of electric for power. Sam Alper's crystal ball was indeed accurate in many ways, so you can see why he had become a success and his vision of future development was very close to the modern day touring caravan.

By the end of 1979 the Ci Group were investing £2 million in the use of computers for production schedules and ordering systems. Production was aimed to be more streamlined, keeping costs down. By 1979 some lucky caravanning kids would own new computer games such as *Tank Warfare* and sports games that were basic by modern times but back then were high tech. The cost of the Colourstars game console (which also ran on battery power) was £39.95, with a cost of up to £19.95 for car racing games. The world of Snap and Snakes & Ladders was changing for the new decade that was approaching.

The tow cars were changing too, and the Ci Tow Car Awards event was set up for the end of the decade – again, and example of Alper's forward thinking. It certainly helped caravanners choose a new car for towing.

Hobby were one of the imports arriving in the UK in the late 1970s.

By this period caravanners wanted improved equipment in their tourer, such as hot water and the shower. There were various makers of water heaters that could be retro fitted, all using gas, such as the Nymph, which could supply a shower or sink and had spark ignition. It was perceived to be easy to fit and economical.

The end of the 1970s had seen innovative designs and construction, but some were too ahead of their time and failed. The touring caravan had progressed from 1970 and in those boom years prices had risen, witnessing a medium-priced popular tourer such as the ABI Ace Pioneer increasing from £451 to £2,016 in 1979.

1970s caravanning was still very much a cheap, value for money holiday, even though caravan prices had risen over the decade. My parents decided as the decade began to draw to a close to stop touring and to buy a static in North Yorkshire. It was a sad day when their last tourer, the Elddis Mistral Silver Jubilee, was dropped off at the dealers. A new 1978 ABI Ace Emperor DEB 28-foot static was the replacement. Sadly Mum passed away twelve months later, but Dad would go on until the 1990s with several statics and, for a while, a seasonal pitched tourer.

The 1970s had seen many changes in caravanning. More folk were going abroad with their tourers and sites in the UK offered better toilet/shower facilities and were adding mains supplies.

There were also new caravan designs and new interiors, and there was a decline of luxury hand-built caravans. 1973 had been the year that a new NCC approved badge was introduced to keep up with NRE requirements in safety. Yet, through the ups and downs caravanning still proved a popular pastime. With more crowded roads, stopping off in a village with the caravan in tow was virtually impossible by this time, with parking restrictions in most beauty spots. Importantly, though, caravanning still represented freedom, holidays and adventure. The next decade would see even more changes, but that's another story!

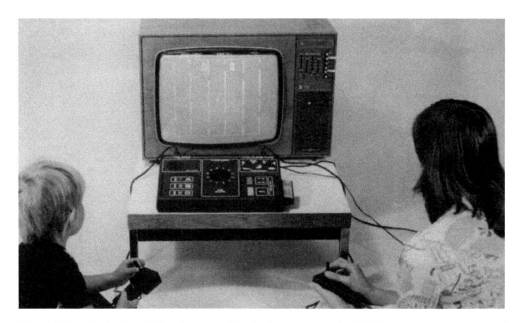

Was this the death of traditional games played when caravanning? This computer game ran off 6-hp2 batteries and popped through the portable.

You'll love the little Nymph's vital statistics.

Above: Hot water in tourers meant having a small boiler unit, like the Nymph, fitted.

Left: The end of the decade would see more mains on sites than were on a coin meter.